Pulling knives from the body to ⬚
deliverance — *The Anatomy of D* ⬚
it's made of; that spit blood on t⬚

the ANATOMY
of DESIRE

: an anthology of distance

selected by Shekinah Vera-Cruz
with an introduction by Valerie Wu

the ANATOMY
of DESIRE

: an anthology of distance

selected by Shekinah Vera-Cruz
with an introduction by Valerie Wu

The Poetry Annals
Oxford, United Kingdom

ISBN 978-0-244-69564-4

Cover & interior layout by Shekinah Vera-Cruz.
Cover image by chuttersnap

Typeset in EB Garamond, Open Sans & Playfair Display.

Printed & bound by Lulu
Published by The Poetry Annals

Email: thepoetryannals@gmail.com
Website: www.thepoetryannals.co.uk

From the vicious, to the clinical, to the confessional, *The Anatomy of Desire* is a collection of poems that cut from where the ache is still tender, and rend longing wide open. Pulling knives from the body to call them holy, crushing berries in fists like deliverance — they ask hunger what it's made of & spit blood on the floor every time they try to speak.

From the vicious, to the clinical, to the confessional, *The Anatomy of Desire* is a collection of poems that cut from where the ache is still tender, and rend longing wide open. Pulling knives from the body to call them holy, crushing berries in fists like deliverance — they ask hunger what it's made of & spit blood on the floor every time they try to speak.

Contents

Editor's Note
by Shekinah Vera-Cruz

In his 1979 collection *Praise*, Robert Hass described desire as "full of endless distances". The configuration, the interpretation, and the eradication of these distances is what this anthology aims to explore. Yet, though we define all longing as the space of tension that lies between any two bodies, the boundaries of desire are difficult to delineate. They are often difficult, even, to imagine or conceptualise. Thus, the works in this collection trace the silhouettes of longing, while they transverse the distance desire implies. They achieve this in ways we hope you will find provocative and enlightening.

However, this collection also aims to cover another distance. In communities, in countries, in a *world*, that is growing increasingly hostile — in which bodies are growing ever further apart — it's our ardent wish that this anthology goes some way towards bridging some great gaps, and bringing people closer together through compassion, generosity, and a common humanity.

Thank you for joining our press in this endeavour. All profits made from the sale of digital and physical copies of this anthology will be donated directly to the international charity *Save the Children*. From the catastrophic famine in Yemen to the horrific separation of families at the United States-Mexico border, *Save the Children* work around the world to preserve and advance the rights of children to good health, safety and education.

We at *The Poetry Annals* are endlessly grateful for the support and contributions of the poets and authors in this anthology. I, personally, am also grateful to everyone who has supported this anthology in any way. From the editors of other presses who advised on a variety of technical matters; to the individuals who helped promote the anthology; to the wonderful authors who produced wonderful blurbs for this book — none of this would have been possible without you. I am also endlessly grateful to *The Poetry Annals* team of Valerie Wu, Christian Summation and Venetta Octavia.

Desire may be full of distances, but at its heart, longing is about shortening them — it is borne of a desire to bring us closer together. We hope that the wonderful art contained within this anthology, and the important work of *Save the Children*, are a step — or several steps — in the right direction.

Shekinah Vera-Cruz
Founder & Editor-in-Chief

Introduction

by Valerie Wu

"Through others, we become ourselves."

This was said by psychologist Lev Vygotsky, who studied the ways interpersonal connection can determine the development of an individual consciousness and thus, the self. Vygotsky's belief was that the earliest conception of identity is shaped through our relationships with others; through the variations in response to unsatisfied desires, a character is formed. From the deepest, darkest parts of human identity to the external parts of it, desire is seen as a form of empathy, of using empathy as a way of seeing others in the lens we use to create ourselves.

The way I think about desire is this: it breathes, but can suffocate. At times it can be a void; at others a lake. It can be violent—an exit wound—or an artery, a means of connection. As such, the poems contained within this anthology dissect the duality of an expressed emotion: the pain it can inflict, but also the subtle ways it can reinforce the memories that have shaped us as much as we have shaped them. In this sense, these poems illustrate the many ways we search for ourselves through others.

For some, desire implies "shared ownership of a program", as Janelle Salanga writes. Functions create values. We look for that value in our lives. Desire is, at its core, a search for intimacy and meaning. Desire is Quinn Lui's "if you knew she heard *prison* when you said *protection*". Desire can be a sentencing; it can reveal the parts of past we choose to keep hidden, an unspoken haunting.

This collection is meant to harbor such narratives in a way that neither glorifies nor shuns, but provides context to an emotion that can be interpreted in a multitude of ways. To look at desire through a personal lens necessitates a self-awareness of the human form. A vessel. A means of forgiveness. The prolonging of a wound, or as Yves Olade writes, a body "broken into pieces". We look at desire as violence, as cutting the meat off bones, but also that desire as a symptom of love, a concept greater than ourselves.

What exists here in the *macro* is a range of poets and poems, each channeling an emotion in their work in many different forms. Yet in the *micro*, what resonates the most within each piece is the way the writers' voices reflect the linguistic way one chooses to translate the process of longing. It is an examination of each organ, each artery, within the human experience and the holiness of hunger. Structurally, these parts each perform different functions, but all are essential to the human body as a whole.

There is a vulnerability present within these poems in that they depict the universality of an emotion so often silenced or stigmatized in society. By understanding desire in all its nuances and complexities, we bear witness to how it functions as a product of not only how we engage with others, but also how we engage with ourselves. These writers invite you to join their stories. We encourage you to explore your own.

Valerie Wu is a student and interdisciplinary writer and artist in the Bay Area, California. She is a two-time National Gold Medalist in the Scholastic Art and Writing Awards and has presented her writing and literary research at Stanford University, the University of California-Los Angeles, and the Asian Art Museum in San Francisco. Her work has been recognized by the National YoungArts Foundation, the Manzanar Awards Committee, and the *Columbia Political Review*, among others.

Inheritance

by Jason Harris

On no sleep my father lived. Went against everything he was
told. Didn't show anything. Ever. I could hear him wail inside
the bathroom at night. I still hear it in my dream. Mouth empty

of teeth & tongue. A spoonful of spice doesn't burn anymore.
When I see him under moonlight petting stray cats, I smile.
Offer him yellow onions, jasmine rice, sockeye salmon, lentil

soup. The last meal he ever cooked he never finished. Be-
hind his apartment complex, when I was twelve, I kissed
a boy. My father caught me & for two long months I bled

into a ceramic bowl. Does not the potter have the right
to shape the clay? My father took me, like a mother takes
her kittens, by the neck & I hung there in the balance

of his strength. In his early fifties he died a drunk who moaned
underneath his breath in ecstasy or shame: *God, I did all I could,
now look at the son you gave me.* His food turned cold & his heart

into a tattered nest in which two sparrows sparred. Be-
fore he died he gave me his wedding ring, his bible,
an apology. Said, on his way out: I loved you like a be-

gotten son. No matter what you think. His final breath:
my mother's name, bird-song, his last & dying will.

[An Analogy of the Body with Rilke]

by Sneha Subramanian Kanta

as though I make my way

like a vein
encased.

so deep inside it
I can't see   any distance:
everything is close

Since I   know enough about pain,
this   makes me small.
you, though—

press down   on me, break in
that I may know   your hand,
and you, the fullness

*an erasure from Rainer Maria Rilke's "III, 1," Book of Hours: Love Poems to God
(translated by Anita Barrows and Joanna Macy)*

Rush Hour Traffic
by Rajani Radhakrishnan

He was something of a brown skinned Basho, maybe the Kerouac
of these roads, a three part poem stuck in rush hour traffic, the

damp ardour of a monsoon morning permeating skin and metal
and silence, everything slick with cologne and sweat and the

after-love of a moment that was two songs long on the FM
radio, a tune stuck diagonally in a brain returning to foreboding

and light, clothes uncrumpled by hands that still trembled, a little,
words unavailable to bridge the distance that minutes ago had

not existed in the tangle of breath and consequence. Even in this
city there are places empty enough for the length of two songs

and one hungry impulse. No endless asphalt here or quiet north
or time for contrition, the unforgiving murmur of the multitude

straightens the doubtful contours of a mistake, stains darkening
on arms, on a lip, a 9 AM haiku, two songs and one lifetime long,

scrawled on a steamy windshield like misspelt graffiti fresh on
peeling walls. I sigh, the taste of the forbidden like a misbegotten

sun in the grey rain. A moment is held up as the day extricates
itself from my limbs. Eight cars wait before us at the toll gate.

This is How We Talk About Desire

by Kwan-Ann Tan

slowly at first, eyes meeting across a darkened
room, orbits intersecting as clumsily but surely
as the way rain falls to earth. porcelain figures
entangled in a dance with too many moves, each
staring down the barrel of the other's
smoking gun. the record-player skipping a beat,
& I am all sensation, honey dripping down
my throat, spine curving towards you
with longing. punch-drunk on our imagined
space as we drive down to the country at
midnight, a careless grin crushing my windpipe
with want. in whispers until you fall asleep in the
backseat, leaving me to memorise the rise & fall
of your shoulder-blades as easily as the
way home. open mouth submitting gently,
without struggle, your hand on my lower back,
heart yearning to call this home.

Unreal

by Rachana Hegde

once I fell slowly to
the bottom of the pool
& the air was chased
from my lips–
this is how I feel
on the dance floor,
spinning into your arms.

*

in an empty room,
an empty song,
there is too much space
to fill with want.
I cannot have the moon
crushed by my longing or
undo the sky like
so much velvet cloth.

*

how convenient
it would have been
to rush through life
& pretend this never happened–

*

in my mind, this moment
has come & passed.
the flowers on the table blush;
you're almost asleep,

head on my shoulder.
I hate that I predicted this,
our small universe
folding into itself.

*

I am carrying you
to the car, the moon
collapsing into slivers
of light, shining
on your mouth,
your hair. I forgot
to ask *is this
what you wanted?*

No More Laurel Trees Until I Have Evaporated

by Marilyn Schotland

Mother, I am sorry for
this disturbance, but a wood

woman told me I have not
learned grace-tongue yet,

so she cursed me to abhor
every green thing that

rips
        the

                earth.
Witch mother,
give me something like

a body. Pretty fused skull,
large hands, & shamed mouth

like Actaeon happening
upon moon-blind Diana.

I'll tell you a secret: he was

happier
        with
                hooves.

These are the eyes I will
wear when my body turns

against me at the age of
twelve. Mother, I deserve

the same: turn me four legs &
plug me with teeth.

Let
                me
                        Fall.

segmentation fault, pit dumped

by Janelle Salanga

sitting here in the darkness,
watching the show we started together,
left unfinished
(you and i)
feeling like a pitted peach. trying to force a system override.
laptop on my thighs
provides the warmth your hands used to.
imagine the darkness, a blank terminal.
(our_relationship.cpp did not compile)
i let you create a directory.
shared ownership of a program, and you warned me:
i am new at this. not prepared. don't know how to (git) commit.
code isn't worth keeping around.
(compile without showing warnings, i said. wanted
your language trailing through mine. wanted to see
two styles smiling back, synthesized as one.)

you dragged green light through,
tapping out functions:
— warm feet shuddering against my cold ones,
tucked next to yours, dwarfed by extra long twin bed.
(e2510: operand size mismatch)
— danced between shifting pedestals of privilege,
you: white, male; me: upper-middle-class,
hashed out uncomfortable, filleted arguments to understand
each other, or to brush against something like understanding.
(e2066: information not available)
— feet against pavement, no bike to race through streets,
just two pairs of footprints, step forward, holding hands,
running after buses, letting my shoes memorize longer strides
just to match yours.
(e2292: function should return a value)

— focused on practice math problems i wrote out for you,
memorialized in the notebook you bought after my eyes jumped to it,
perched on that same bed, alternating scribbles and mac & cheese,
took peeks at you from the corner of my eye, caressed the periphery.
(e2023: array of references is not allowed)
— it's not you, it's me, you would've been the right person
for a different time / person / me,
facetime and the heartbreak so loud i swear
you can hear it through the screen.
(e2450: undefined structure 'structure')

and i dipped my fingers into syntax
swirled it around,
came up with one last function,
this one the pit:
— i love you, present tense
(e2040: declaration terminated incorrectly)

sorry.
past tense. i mean past tense.
i mean to say, i don't want you back
but i hate how much the memories sting.
how sweet turns sour.
how i can't close the terminal, delete the program,
override the conversations we layered over episodes
of this show / months of my life,
now just pits in my heart.
can't bite into a peach / write a new program
without thinking of you,
juice dribbling down, residues of
something almost like love
sticking into skin,
functions working again.

Psalm 7

by Aaron White

Of strange people

¹Springs, rushing torrents
  O God, you cut openings.
²There are pools of blood.
   There is sugar water in my mouth.
³My blood, it oozes into honey,
   into nectar, O God
⁴They drink it. They drink and
   it sustains them.
⁵These worthless, wicked people,
   they drain my lips of color
⁶And pucker from the taste
   of bitter wormwood.
⁷When they reject my sweetness,
   shun the respite, O God
⁸They tear at me like lions, they tear
   my robe, my flesh,
⁹Pervert my words with those
   crooked organs, their tongues.
¹⁰You crushed the heads of
   Leviathan, O God,
¹¹And you watch my nation
   conspire, you watch
¹²My nation plot in vain.
   O, these wicked people,
¹³They wink and wax pleasant when
   they unleash rape and death,
¹⁴Set fire to your sanctuaries. These
   birds snagged by their own snares
¹⁵O God, they say truth is
   not truth.

¹⁶But I know their throats
        are open graves
¹⁷That stretch from Heaven
        to Earth, their tongues
¹⁸Range over the earth and
        Threaten to swallow us all
¹⁹Alive while spewing Proverbs
        without understanding that
²⁰Wisdom begins with getting wisdom.
        Whatever else is merely insight.
²¹O God, I am so tired.
        I am weary with moaning.
²²And although the wicked colonize
        my mouth, I will sing.

                Selah

²³I will prowl as the wicked
        prowl but exalt Psalm.
²⁴I will sing as I fulfil
        every vow we have made, even
²⁵As wicked teeth sink into my flesh
        and pierce my liver.

                Selah

²⁶They will trade our silver
        with flattering talk,
²⁷Spurn our crowns of beauty
        and piss in our Egyptian linen
²⁸Once sweetened with cinnamon,
        aloe, myrrh.

                Selah

²⁹They may take us and our ways
        as shrewd, or strange,
³⁰But we are not shrewd, nor
        are we senseless.

                Selah

³¹We contain multitudes. We know
        that as they uproot our roads

[32]They are paving short paths
        to Sheol.

[33]I know those who hate us,
        they love Death.
[34]Those lovers of lovers of violence,
        they take
[35]Death as a lover. They
        embrace fire.

When You See the Videos

by Kevin A. Risner

of the last decade
innocence grew like the sunset
pink & neon blue hopscotches
butterscotch suckers stuck to birches

we ran to the tracks when we heard the whistle
we watched the engine belch past us
& our minds did not go to videos
like the ones we watched in eighth grade

people behind fences & boxcars trundling by
to the next concentration camp
the next cage exists
down towards the border

new people are being kept there
just for a little while, they say
but the tang of the pollen is coming
from elsewhere

does the pollen fly over the southern border
we can tell by sucking in the air
does it yearn to go back
to where it came from

there's nothing back there for some people
there was everything here at the horizon
but that everything disappeared instantly
as together they were gone

if leaving they won't survive
if staying they will be locked up
with those already here
in the land of the free

& the home of the brave
who doesn't flinch when they see
wailing voices or vacant stares
blinks by a four-year-old

who asks
what is the middle ground here
when you see that this is
happening again & again

In which the waiting girl stops listening to static

by Mary Sims

1.

Half-formed girl peeling back
these letters in rows of hungry
tongues learns

what takes from the light when
you are nothing but it & not to
let these walls catch what's

left. Angel face likes to yell about
hell fire & how pretty you look
dressed in it— driving down

this road like there's nowhere
left to go. Just you & them &
that glass eye following every

where. How you see it between
you & how it's screaming, *turn
back* at every exit. Laughing

about how caught means there
must be something *hidden, first*
when you take the curb.

2.

A bird asks a waitress in a diner
are there any seeds here? and the
waitress says, *none you didn't sew
yourself*   & laughs.

& so it's back to the window. Back
to watching the bird scramble for what
what isn't there between red leather
seats with the waitress chanting

*you're never going to find it. you're
never going to find it. you're never
going to—*

          Back to the bird sifting through all
          the barren seeds,
                    waiting to see
          what falls from their   shells.

3.

There's a lot of ways to learn starvation,
so you look at that mouth & cross *five* on
to your arm. A bruised bumble girl in all

this skin & after a while it starts to beat
into want.

Tally marks leave themselves in place
of what's missing & still refuses to show
itself.   There's a million ways to write

desire & you are missing
          all of them. You learn it in how

Angel face likes their things better bruised & watch
as the bird comes back— scratching the story out

onto your thighs
                    like a scripture there's no
translation for.

Those red leather diner seats take what's left
of all that light with them & you watch that
glass eye watching back— waiting for all
the bird's teeth to stop coming in so
                                    sharp.

blood moon

by Quinn Lui

a reprimand: how unscientific this is.
candlelight chosen for how it trembles,
uncertain as your pulse. how it masks
the rot and its humming heat, but

counterpoint: corpse-coldness. when
you exhaled like you'd meant to drown
and the lake bloomed poppy-red. when
the moon slipped away, siren-smooth,
and fit herself under your fingernails like

an accusation. your eyes brim with it
and she won't apologize but she might promise
to do a better job of wiping the blood off
next time — next time, she'll skip from history
to ghost story. leave the legend
sleeping with the memory, leave

the confession. so of course it comes back
to wrists and throats, those parts that split
and fishbellied up in the half-light.
it comes back to lips and eyes, and skin,
always skin, flushed with apology and numb
with the morning cold. it comes to

setbacks; her asking if you wanted to wrap her
in cotton wool. if you knew she heard *prison*
when you said *protection*. if you knew
her temper was not hair-trigger but kept
in the space between point of impact
and the tip of the weapon, every motion

a sentencing. listen: if death is at the door
she will offer your body. eyes closed
as the wetness wells up in every socket.
back straight as the morning light
slants into something like regret.

roanoke
by Amrita Chakraborty

wednesday, three horses
thundered past me in the night   their hooves

    hard like weeping   they were black or   maybe the sootstruck vespers

made   their flowing bodies so   i   reached my hand out   and horsehair
    brushed   then fell away   from me.

why can i not   haunt you like this why can i not will these fingers into   talons

why these   eyes   not spectral vehicles   the horses   passed me but only after
they took

      me deep   into my sordid body. when you   deliver death payment
  for her services   will you sign my name on the check. my, what violence
i bid her   visit upon   the only
        only ones kind enough to cage me. yes lalita,

i am mad. madly, i kiss the stone out of the man. lalita, spell it out

on this tree. in the night, they ride again their hooves into hands shall read our
    story
  then   gather us up bear us out to their shadowed grove, all transformed.

Tender Aphrodite She Has Almost Killed Me

by Logan February

after Sappho

Gasp — the hiss of the soda.

It is morning, he is next to you.
CGI handsome. Dream-dappled & drinking

a Coke. A wicked vision: he stuns you

& o, that he would hold you in this summer heat,
his pulse against the curve of you, your sweat, just so.

You wake to him with a Coke in his hand —

of course you gasp. You had dreamed you were
one of his cold Cokes. He popped the red can.

When the froth of you came, he licked.

reeling in, letting go

by S. A. Khanum

through the wilds of prayer & gluttony
by your fingers & hair & mouth

down your throat, a wild litany

...

shame hangs a bloated moon, everywhere
I walk, she follows

by my hands, a wolf, by my tongue, distance

...

it is in arctic rivers you'll follow me
under pink skies, we'll steal our last breaths

but before we go under, we'll wait

& when they come
we'll peel back our own skins

& when your eyes gill my ribs
my heart will pluck a moon from your eyes

...

& shame is shame is love & to love is to forgive

& I say

sink into the blue
revel in the things that make you undone

Scrapes

by Wanda Deglane

after Naomi Washer

this is a photo of me, but happy. this is a photo of me, but with healthy coping skills and no lasting trauma. this is a photo of the sandbox where I fell and skinned my knees and elbows. these are the friends who took me to the bathroom to mop up the scrapes with cheap toilet paper, this is how much I loved them. this is the overwhelming, soul-crushing feeling that they never loved me back. this is the house I always passed on my way home from school, the big white one with the green shutters I pictured myself living in one day, before someone painted it beige and later tore it down. this is a photo of every hope I had, brilliant and colorful before someone painted them beige and later tore them down. this is a photo of my first dog, the little huff he'd make every time he'd plop down at my feet. this is my guilt when I forgot to say *I love you* the last time I saw him alive. this is the interstate winding up and down over the hills heading north, how I sat in the back of my mom's minivan and pretended they were roller coasters. this is a photo of me blasting Gwen Stefani's Sweet Escape on the road to Flagstaff, my brother singing the 'woohoos' while I sing the 'yeehoos.' this is the first boy I ever kissed at thirteen, my teeth crashing into his braces like a fiery train collision. there he is violently pawing my just-budding boobs while I try to teach myself to say no. this is a photo of everyone I've ever loved. the boy who sang me to sleep. the girl with the ukulele. the boy who tried to rape me. this is a photo of my body, fifteen years old and naked, lying petrified. this is a photo of my body, sixteen years old and emaciated, all the fat sucked from my razor bones, sharp like a weapon. this is a photo of my body, seventeen years old and destroyed, bruised in some places and raw in others. this is a photo of me, forcing myself to write a happy poem and then derailing halfway through. this is a photo of every embarrassing thing I ever said, and how it would haunt me five, ten, fifteen years after. this is every shitty thing no one's apologized to me for, how I strangled every drop of truth from the earth looking for closure. this is me killing all the past versions of myself and calling it closure. this is the truth that closure's a fucking myth. this is the truth that no one can ever love you enough to save you. this is a photo of the first house I ever lived in, and my room with the lavender walls and the TV where I tried to shove crayons inside the VCR slot. this is the room now, painted a sickly yellow, the TV lying in a dump a hundred miles away. this is a photo of my father beating my mother in front of me. this is a photo of my father beating my mother in front of me. this is a photo of my father beating my mother in front of me. here I am begging her to file a restraining order against him to make up for the shame I feel for every time I would tell myself, *the next time, I will stop him. the next time, I will step in,* yet the next time my entire soul went numb, like the shrill deafness after an explosion, and I did nothing. this is a photo of cotton candy ice cream from Baskin-Robbins. this is a homecoming dress, stained with spaghetti sauce and tears. this is a photo of every boy who told me, *you're so different from all the other girls.* this is a photo of every girl who ever said my hair looked like a bees' nest. this is my hair now, still all stingers and honey. this is a photo of me at four, dark pigtails and Mary Janes, trying to teach myself how to hula hoop. this is a photo of me at nearly twenty. I still don't know how to fucking hula hoop. this is a photo of me, with every half-forgotten memory, with all the tears and laughter stitched into my skin. this is a photo of me. I am falling through broken mirrors. I am forgiving myself.

MY TIMELINE IS GLAD

by stephanie roberts

Michelle Williams is married and in love.
Joy slops through the gaps of chronological anarchy
in a corporately motivated timeline algorithm;
I manage to put one and one together.
My timeline is usually enraged or aggrieved:
school shooting, tasered Black school girl,
another brown skinned citizen getting
the death penalty, on camera, without trial.
Today the crowd rejoices, wishes her well,
in some cases tearfully. More power to her,
or whatever it is the chirren say.
Get it sis (finger snaps).
We all want to cozy to redemption, not poetic all
literal all. Redemption, restoration, love. I believe,
I want to believe! Michelle, help me my unbelief!

Taking photos of flowers, in belligerent July,
I trap the blue iridescence of a small lepidopteran.
Female, Karner blue, *P. melissa*, "locally extinct."
Show her a picture of herself,
mouth part filling heart with nectar,
where she is not supposed to exist. Michelle,
how is she here? How did she survive
the loss of home her desire? We gave up too soon
—*locally extinct*. Mouth draw sweet.
She didn't know she was finished
so she wasn't.

Cafuné

by Saoirse

I told her hair did not matter
Kissed her bald head good
—bye

...

Found a lock of hair
Pressed between the pages of a story
she left unfinished
Holding her place
Waiting for her
to resume their journey together

...

Spent all day with
the silken placeholder in my grasp
I couldn't turn the page.

what is love but an animal with its face buried deep in the ground?

by Jason Harris

tonight, i feel as if my heart might stop, but i am not certain. certain i
am of only a few things tonight: of the moth that flies toward light, of

the gnats wine-soaked & dead, that love is simply love & nothing else, that a day
before you left, i was headed south which is to say: away from home, away

from all & whom i love. sometimes, when i'm alone, to myself I repeat a
thing so intimate it undresses before it leaves my mouth: *come back*. i am

uncertain that i know anything: how to comfort you in distress, the true
distance between *affect* & *effect*, exactly what my heart is doing, or

what is on the other side of the dark blue sky. love is simply love. nothing
else. this, my one, is my undoing. & *this*, my one, is a love poem &

nothing else. what does it matter if it takes a plane to get to you? or
that the heart always lives up to its hype? or that the sky is luminous &

black & beyond the dark blue our prayers gaslight the stars? tonight, i feel
as if my heart might stop & i am certain the moth flying toward the light

& the gnats wine-drunk & dead, whispering *Jason*, knows something I don't.

Some Divine Law for Desire

by Mateo Lara

for Mark

Yes, I will ask for grace. This is the millionth time.
& wait, you can't talk about the light—like that, with all that love.
Pero, come over here, drag out this hurt, drag it out & suck on it
Put ice on bruised arm, burnt flesh, possess me with wicked intent
Or nah, nevermind, chulo, just be rough, God will forgive us some other day.

I can't empower myself right now, the gringo had me calling him last night
What's that? Three times in one month, fuck, I've lost my mind
drew back curtain in dark cave and now I'm restless.

What is resistance? It is pulling covers when sun is up
Wound prolonging, I can't tell grandma this, what pain is
The big words make no sense
She'll go on with all that chisme between her lips
Gather rot & wood penetrating blistering skin.
come approach me in a meaningless manner, but with meaning
make it mean a little more while God looks down
your white God, not mine.

Pero no virgin could hold my purity & save this routine so endless
of searching for routine, an epiphany okay, fine I'll hold my hands out
what were the words again?
Don't call me stupid, don't call me fool
Jesus died for my already-done-with sins
And that's bible, go on
& yes, get mad—I already said my prayers.

A Ghazal for Our Romance with References to the Color Blue

by Sneha Subramanian Kanta

for H

I have held you in a thousand different births. You are the color blue,
like breaths of the Pacific. I inherit your love—a shade of underwater blue.

We walk the museum with its sarcophagus relics. We stop by a stupa
where the window overlooks anemones. Your body grows in the blue

light of aubade. In a quiet church, we spot a corner where parakeets sing
with peaceful silences in our interludes, as large windowpanes painted blue.

Yesterday you patted a bird on its neck. A bird with feathers as blue hydrangeas.
We tune into the ocean at evening with a compass pointing toward the blue.

You are a book of hymns opened into the wide expanse of wavering tides.
I see gloaming descend onto our faces with shadows of solidifying blue.

Summer Viper

by S. K. Grout

the ancient greek word of the day is dakethumos // I wake in a sweat, why is it twenty degrees with the window closed // on the other side of the fire, the female monster removes the head of the hero // did I get that right // sometimes a needle brings you closer to god // a full circle of blood // a sword strapped on // blood the colour of myth // ink // that's right // last night, before I fell asleep, anne carson told me // men want to stopper up all my lips // a life of boiling silence // poor snake headed lady, it is me that loves you // did I get that right // my bedroom cloaks in heat // your body is bone-strung, skin bare // snakes being nocturnal animals, becalm in 8AM sun, your love free // that's right // you already sculpt the light with strike // the heat makes me want to go right back to sleep, but I cannot // heart-vexed // did I get that right?

Police Report Regarding My Father

by Wanda Deglane

2 AM. night crisp as firewood in late August.
VICTIM opens the front door slowly,
carefully, like she's expecting hail storms,
her face half shadow like chiaroscuro. in
the light of the kitchen, VICTIM looks as if
she's been crying but also bleeding. OFFICER
takes pictures of her mangled face, her lips
torn and nose still pouring blood. OFFICER
asks what happened, and VICTIM speaks
quickly in a broken accent. she came home
late. turned on the kitchen light and there
he was. the downpour lasted eight minutes,
each second dragging itself on its stomach,
and the baseball bat she seized from the
garage did nothing to save her. SUSPECT
saw her reach for the phone and fled in a gold
sedan. he sits under humming gas station lights,
his knuckles raw as stinking summer heat
against his steering wheel. (when OFFICER
finds him weeks later, he sweeps away the
photographs like a mosquito, like an
inconvenience. *I don't know how her face got
like that. but it looks like she may have learned
her lesson.* OFFICER drives home to his own
wife that night, his skin crawling.) VICTIM
covers her mouth to smother her own sobs,
says she doesn't want to wake her kids. she
looks up to the heavens, dark and empty, like
she's pleading. OFFICER turns, tries to see what
vision she sees, and finds the stars fizzling
out as if the sky is falling unconscious. in the
distance, he finally hears children wailing.
VICTIM raises her hands, trembling, screaming,
where were you, god. where were you

Resemblances to the Sun

by Nicole Yurcaba

My cousin
sends photos
of Spain's green pigeons.
She writes
My new boyfriend
doesn't understand me.

When I read this,
I giggle, girlish & gaping,
remembering my grandmother's
admonition: *Anna Marichka,*
you always be misunderstood.

My cousin
laments her
loss: Serhiy,
her first husband,
with the tiny apartment
who brought her mother bread.

I empathize—the man who
read my eyes & face
withered: a willow
ripped from the river's bank.

He cherished
my roughshod tongue,
my Cyrillic skin, cleansed
in Kupala night's
bonfire.

*My new boyfriend works
in marketing,* my cousin
writes. *He treats me
like a magazine ad.*

Years ago, my grandmother read
Frost's "Fire and Ice,"
asked me how I thought
the world will end. Instead,
I posed *But, Baba, am I beautiful
enough for a man to love?*

In response to my cousin,
I write *Kuzyna, you are
more than a face on glossed
paper. Tell your new boyfriend
to read our history, some Shevchenko,*

*Kostenko, Zabuzhko, & if he
can crack the mystery of us,
keep him. Otherwise,
remain the black and red crosses
forming roses & poppies
on our vyshyvanka.*

Before she died, grandmother told me
of sunflowers as tall
as determined
as God.
She said *Remember
the earth from which you came.*

Remember, the greatest bloom
occurs after the earth has scorched.
Someday, a man will turn for you
as the sunflowers turn for the sun.
My cousin continues
with questions:
my impending wedding? A vacation
east? An observation that I planted
four dozen sunflowers facing
west— *Why west?*
I tell her I would have
planted more; in any direction,
with sunflowers,
there are never enough.

Chelsie's Prayer

by Chandler Veilleux

Battleboro, Vermont

Bless me, Chandler, for I have sinned. This is my first confession:

I am a nail-biter. I am left-handed.   I am guilty of doubt.
I can become a ghost just like   — that.
I believed my mother when she said   *You will always be Chelsie.*

Chandler,   I want to tell you about the times I have made
myself invisible   without inviting that blindness back inside.
You are stronger than me.   You will carry us to the finish line,
I know it.   But these are the things I still have to answer for:

my dirty fingers   my chewed-up cheeks   the bitterness that blooms so well
the time I hid under the blankets   while my sister was sobbing at the door
the look on my wife's face   when she said   *I feel like you haven't loved me in ages*
how I had been counting on that recognition   how   across the checkered table
of a rest stop coffee shop   I said   *You're absolutely right.*

Chandler,   I don't know how to reconcile the space between us.   I am small.
I fold too easily.   Healing takes so long   and   I am afraid
that you're not coming —   that I am waiting   to tear out of my dungeon
only to become a sequel   to this story: *Hold tight.   I am on my way.*

Chandler,   I am dreaming of the day you save me from these heavy places:
the day when   my hands will become your hands   and   you'll unlock
the echelon of sweet flowers   and   fuse all the synapses between
being *a stranger*   and   being *a home.*

Chandler,   I can see your shadow across the bridge.   It's a miracle
we've made it this far.   Please: give me the strength to go just
a little bit further.   Hold my hand until we safely cross.   And then,

lay me down   in the green pastures
lead me along   the still waters

reach out to me   show me your face
baptize me   in your laugh —

I've been dying to hear it.

TRAUMA GUIDE TO GUNSHOT WOUNDS
by Yves Olade

in the end i took it all · with my mouth undone · and my head tipped back · your thumb
blooming bruise · waxing wound · on my jaw · told me to open up · so i cracked up wide ·
took communion like a shot · and didn't even taste the blood · just felt the burn going
down · fire i couldn't · choke back up · so every night · for a week · I spat lead · into my
palms · and it didn't mean anything · it didn't matter at all · only proved that · like a bullet
· confession · can't be held behind the teeth · only fired from the throat · into whatever is
waiting · absolution in exchange · for doing unto others · what they have always done
unto you · but violence · like trauma · is always wider · on the other side · we write elegies ·
to the exit wound · but pain is still · the shortest distance · between two bodies · is still the
only ghost · between the human and divine · and in trying to haunt the distance · i turned
the chamber · of a gun · into a bottle · and asked · for its truth · but found death · instead ·
swinging · from its own cross · and singing vicious hymns · i learnt that · liturgy's lesson ·
so i no longer care · to throw myself from buildings · to wonder at what · i could survive ·
if given the opportunity · like every good martyr · i now know · that at the end · of every
fall · is another barrel · to look down · to beg God · to be delivered from · the heart beating
· out a prayer · the blood becoming · its own sacrament · the body broken · into pieces ·
small enough · to consume but · not enough · to satisfy.

Substitute for the Still God

by Amrita Chakraborty

Call it what you want.
A flame veering into a field.

A sun searching for its double,
discus-ing till heat envelops

the latch. The lick of pursuit
as birds sight the scattered fruit.

Hunt me if you like.
I've grown sick of abstaining,

of sharpening this body like a
holy sword. There were once

ten thousand shining behind me,
my flag burnt copper at the edges

yet vivid against our stockpiled silt.
You could follow me too—

Be the bull in red. For me,
the bluish rip current, wheeling

into reach. For you, I'll be that still
god. I'll be your vital clearing.

My palms your beacon in the exodus,
your vision mine in what comes next.

American Queer Arrives Late To Blind Date

by Sage

The reality is, the catastrophe of missed connections
Lies not in the passing of two lonely bodies orbiting
Each other in a coffee shop or used-book store, but
In the glance of want I should be saving for my love
But cannot help giving out like desperate adverts for
Attention in an arid field of reap-less fruit. I've culled
Every twig-boned boy from my past. Look at the buds
Growing from each skinned knee I touch. I leave legs
Spread wide like a maiden leaves monsters weeping
For her sleeve. I leave a wake of barrel-chested men
Scratching at their heads to catch a glimpse of my goods.
All the good in the world couldn't spare them from my teeth.
All the good I have to give's been taken, left by the river
In the hands of a boy too thirsty to know that here, he can drink.

half past nine

by S. K. Grout

after Anna Akhmatova

half past nine, suburbia's corner. gum-streaked pavement
underneath, my phone speeding time.

people and foxes on the move around me. my head is tipped.
the moon whips the sky into cigarette remains.

I see stars but I cannot measure the weight of light when I am waiting
for you. without you standing here, they could be satellite stations.

every street lamp could be falling. I draw the word f r i e n d into the air
with an index finger. slightly sweaty, no audience,

it makes a haphazard rhythm, swallowed whole. such a small moment
for a code only you can break. around your finger is a ring,

mother of pearl inlay, worn only at night, a place of waiting.
is it walking its way to me? when we meet, we will set aside

the street-clamour to understand the breeze's voice.

[friend, a hidden word]
[your visit, swapping selves]
[look, she's coming]

the shimmer of battle just outside the gaze,
but there, nevertheless.

Reclamation, Two Years Later

by Kanika Lawton

You told everyone you always leave
at least one internal back door open; an exit
plan, fire escape, running backstage before
the jeers start rising. You made it easy for
yourself. "Hint at long-term commitment in

order to secure short-term affection,"
which means my body, shattered but standing.

When you asked me to lean against the window,
naked, face towards the LA skyline, of course
I said yes. Of course I thought you were splitting
from the way I made you pulse,

hands a better lover than I will ever be, my mouth
a close second.

I called myself innocent. Forgot her face as quickly
as I learned her name. Made note of the hunger
in your texts and the ring on her hand. Forgave
myself for not telling her. Lied. Prayed she is happy.
Lied.

Remembered what you called yourself, after the
wedding, after you've cleaned your head of me—

"I was a coward."

Little Tadpoles

by Manahil Bandukwala

Black sharpie, drawn lines
always hidden for bigger spectacle

future to strive for. To evade
battering of skipped stones.

One lucky enough to slip away. Another
slips under rock. Future frog, unsuccessful

one lives on. We're here for the morality.
To know that retreating to nature means something

for us. That the drumming in the distance
isn't just a warning. Certain sounds evoke

a flow. Fireworks on nights
when you only want quiet.

Incision

by Elizabeth Ruth Deyro

cut my chest   open and see

if my heart still looks like a   heart. i lost count of how often

i had to reconstruct it after watching   it crash against concrete and fall apart.

i am no cultural caricature but i try to be.   biology laughs at how much we worship

false effigies of the heart, how invested we are on the lie that somewhere between arteries are names

of everyone we have ever loved. yet we keep loving, happily convincing ourselves that a heart is only

a heart when two sides merge as one, existing to complete one another. tell me how to find *happiness*

because i heard that *survival* is the only way. i never knew what *love* is until i saw two people merge

as one, existing to complete one another. two men kiss in front of a church, i watched them find

happiness through survival. cut my chest open and let me know if i am still capable of loving

the same way, naked and willing. i lost count of how often i had to scratch out names of

everyone i used to think i loved. the mistakes were never worth the vandalism, but i

heard that *love* was synonymous to *gamble*. i gambled and lost more than i ever

invested. perhaps *redemption* means *to play safe*. i try to build my walls

as high as i can, until his eyes met mine and i began to wonder if

my frayed edges would fit well with his. and i know that *love*

existed solely in thought, that *love* is not worth falling

apart for, but he said perhaps *redemption*

means to *start over*, that *love* is worth

the risk for a shot at *happiness*. i

ask, cut my chest open and

carve his name on

what is left of

Me.

Woman With Fake Emeralds

by Logan February

It was familiar music, so I smiled.
Eyed the burning candles until
They burned into little glowing dots.
A blurry-but-perfect picture, so perfect
With His holy light pouring into
A woman's fake emeralds. I wondered:

Does she wish they were real emeralds?
Or is she content? Because that *is*
A lovely little earring, sitting
At the side of her lovely little neck.
And her ear itself, it was hearing
The same music that was making me smile.

I knew why I was smiling, but
Why was *she* smiling, when the song meant
Please, God, please, God, please, God,
How was her comfort found in begging?
That was when I knew that the woman
Must wish the fake emeralds on her ears

Were real emeralds. So she has a void too!
I was pleased to hear the echo.
I felt the emptiness grow more empty.
Inside that emptiness, there were
Four candles making a perfect picture.
It was blurry because I watching

Through my old eyes again.
But really, it was so perfect,
Even when the woman joined the line
For a sip of His blood.
Even though she wished it was real blood
It was a perfect picture in my mind.

Who Makes You Feel Safe Will Not be Found

by Jen Rouse

The scream is slow
to form
at my lips—though she
is faceless and
restless, though she
pins me
to the bed and rips
the soul from
my throat. And I watch
myself watch myself
as I suffocate
in her mouth. (I wanted her
mouth to save
me once. At the same time
every Tuesday.)
She swallows me
whole. *Huh*, I think,
in that unearthly space
where the body slips
from the body, in that
unholy moment
where the undoing
is done, *fuck it,*
I will not
go this time.

Here is my hand
reaching out from
inside her mouth.
Here is the way
I will pull myself
out and shed
the shell of her.
Here is how I
will take her head
in my hands, her lips
to my lips. Here is how
I will do this, having
always been
done to.

Immaculate Acres

by Elisávet Makridis

for Pappou

Once, on the eve of the Heart's
new-thick imperium, God happened.
Immaculate acres of rare liquid
started to rush like a good racing horse.
You are lucky not to be afraid of dying,
no speck of gorgeous hesitation
on your tongue. You keep the door ajar.
The well-lit paddocks of your life,
clearing overnight. Warp in the mirror
like a weary mirage. You've come this far,
out of sheer kismet. When the moment draws
do not wait to dip your head in. Do not
apologize mid-plummet. Didn't I hear you
tell me you wanted the moon to be a moon
again? Not this diorama of tack-edged
hands airing your wardrobe, piece by piece.
Don't bother to make the bed. You've a soul
as stark as a firm baptism. The summer is
full of nightingales leaving us. Lay down
your impeccable, white-haired longing.
You are lucky not to be afraid.

death of a boyband

by Amy Kinsman

that's it then. the band broke up
    and offer now
        a pill for the small griefs:

    some bittersweet melody;
        some distant smile played on repeat;
    those soft doe-eyes dust-sheeted as your love turns
        to face away.

            this is rehearsal,
        you come to learn,
            for the next performance.

candle snuffed
  so a bonfire knows how to burn itself out -
and you will mix the tincture
    just right when the moment arrives,
but for now you satisfy your need for hurt,
  some bubbling undercurrent not yet heard,
sobbing into lemonade.

they're made to measure boys
    custom built to fill the hollow void as your hand
first grasps the air.
      your choice of five, or six,
  to fit your preference.
      so you select a favourite,

        that first ache
    sugarspun
      from his lips,
        tooth-rot stuff.

it never lasts.
boyhood
    gives way to man,
    puppy fat undressed,
        how tease
            moves on to boldness
    and you dance along,
        a beat or two behind.

                    they'll always leave you,
                    outgrow the baby steps -
                        change their hair, their genre -
                    pick up a guitar, an addiction, disappear.

and it hurts
        at least as far as you can understand,
    tears on your pillow and all those grand clichés
            played out unironically
                    as you rip the posters from the wall,
                break cds over your skinny little knees,
            shriek and wail
                for their betrayal.

                    practice pain
                    for the real thing.

Can You Say Amen

by Sage

After your throat opens the sky
the way a jaguar opens the peccary's
              swollen belly on a riverbank in Paraguay's

Gran Chaco, after your hand cups
my lap slide guitar during the Neo Show
              live at the Apollo concert hall, after

my father could pray again to the god
of my mother. I love how you can pray
              to the god of all your mothers.

I love you for that. I know sometimes
your legs get tired trying to carry so much grief.
              Centuries and centuries

holding us bound—together, yes, but
separated from the wider expanse of
              everything we've ever called the sea:

A mother's embrace. A father's distance.
The mystery of what comes after earth
              (whether another planet or a different realm

or perhaps the great bleached ribs of a god
jutting from the mossy ground like the ruins
              of chapels scattered across the highveld).

I know sometimes you like to look out the
airplane window and imagine all those clouds
              inside your lungs. What I would give to be

those clouds. To be as close to your heartbeat
as possible. This lifetime is conducive to love
            the way my past life was conducive to loneliness.

You give me each day as if it's yours to give.
Look at the shadow of the trees on the dunes;
            it does not mean an end, but it belongs to us alone.

if we were taller do you think we'd shave less; kiss less; lose less

by Allegra Lisa

for a friend and his cats

if we were anything more than the skin our mothers slept in
when they were young and sober, we'd stop sticking

to the things that liquored up little boys and their toy trucks; we'd be rising sons.
if i could paint you, i'd line your brow

with everything that tasted purple. i'd tell you i feared the way
your lips stumbled over white teeth balancing on the edge of your coffee

mug on sunday afternoons. i'd tell you i loved you
and the patches you've pressed into your hats and ankles more than i loved trying

to fix broken men and their fast fingers. if i were a mother, i'd make sure
this never happened to mine. if i could find you,

i'd ask you to stop him from falling
apart on the floor in front of me. i'd tell you it was lilies that swallowed

our last bent reflection; that it was prettier things that forced their way
into the grooves of our thumbs.

Line Breaks

by S. K. Grout

We're reading cruel novels between each other, you one side of the battered, paisley couch, me the other, this site of hosted paragraphs. An apricot carnation in a vase pinned to the wall above us, drinking water. You picked it from the neighbour's garden at dawn. I didn't watch but I lay in bed imagining it. Your wicked stealth. Your steaming cut. The way you lingered in the garden, smirked at the window. The grasp of summer only tentative. You're wearing ruffles. No watch. I make my body a lake around you, I contort my body to sew eye contact. My hand a fist of your dress. That goes on and on, that heartbeat. You're dissatisfied with the hero's arc, the beats per minute, the lack of purpose, the lover's unwashed hair. Tomorrow we will be glass fragments, no pages to turn. Your dress a blue of all the places we will never go. My eyes unsaving us. You expect my heart to over-eat, but what is love but a sundress, a choose-your-own adventure, an unchartered galaxy. It is me that keeps the time.

Ghazal for an Endoscopy of Cities

by Sneha Subramanian Kanta

Mumbai

You've thought about how human beings get endoscopies taken but not cities.
You examined the arteries of your city like a doctor with sharp eyes. Cities

roar in emptiness, growl when a fullness overcomes them. Landscapes, cities.
Some say the ocean that passes through this city makes it unlike other cities.

It reminds them of Moby Dick—they set out like voyagers in quest of ocean cities.
You know this city has an undesirable itch for its grayscale concrete. Hues, cities.

This city has a sugar-glazed exterior for the unfamiliar ones. New cities
burgeon in hopes to compare to its throbbing pulse. But you know how cities

tire, like human beings. The city with its bone crypts, cries like more cities
might be—you see the city vomit toxic leftovers. A residue memory, cities.

Bell Jar Saviour
by Sherry Bollero

On days when the odd shaped
bitter moons let me slip through the cracks to Cerberus
those little white stacks of skulls
dissolve in the frothing sea.

When the pyre is stacked high
nine lives dwindle down by one—
the silver soft worms multiply
across the skin, crumbling through the chambers a charred heart.

I can be so still in the garden of my failed attempts
among all the bright blooms, each a breath—
prayer to the woman who cut Her feet down this pebbled way,
left streamers of too-red tulips twisting into the fig trees.

Hell begs at my heels, She says, *stealing scraps of me at a time.*
The sound of getting thinner
echoes off the shores of my ears. But She is busy
pulling words like petals from the devil's lips. Laughing wild at her solitary work.

I'm inept at this perfected art; it isn't for me.
I iron out the greying linen of my travails, hang it
near the late burning fire— dream
away from the beginning of my last breath, once more

Rise, like Lazarus,
leave the grave of my bed— scatter the flower sheets to the floor,
devour the morning air. For taking my turn
I praise Sylvia, listen to *I am*,

stay out of the kitchen

Lavender fury

by Brittany Coppla

i learned to find comfort
in your limp hug
around the sobering white
of a toilet seat,

because the friday night
flush of your cheek
pressed against its porcelain
meant your fury was exhausted.

this time, it wasn't even midnight.

it was hard to read
your february eyes, no more
than bloodshot slits.

the safety of your latched doorknob
offered more metallic tenderness
than the aluminum of a beer can

and in the harsh light of your bathroom,
i watched sporadic tears drip,
then plummet into the plumbing.

i wondered if your relentless search
for a sense of self, an understanding
of your own name,
was the cause of your eyes' unforgiving glaze
(but know it was just Jack Daniels
making himself known).

against the sickly pale of your skin,
the bags beneath your eyes
seemed a little darker.
but maybe that is because
you expect them to carry so much.

when i think of that night,
i try to remember that
i had brought a pillow from your bedroom
to cushion my head against the tile
while my palm traced circles on your back.

the last thing before
descending into sleep
was the smell of navy blue:
like the back of your neck
and lilac detergent.

it's Sunday, today (my favorite day of the week
for rain) and i think:
you are merely suspended somewhere
between lavender and fury.

Hypnosis

by Sean Glatch

I heard somewhere that a mother will kill someone under hypnosis
if she's convinced they're a threat to her child.
I didn't believe it, really,

but lately I'm not so sure. I've been dangling my sexuality
in front of my mother's eyes like a stopwatch, time dropping off of its hands

like rotting fruit, and I wonder, when I run out of time to hide my identity, will my
queerness look like a monster pressing its claws in her son's throat?
And will my mother respond as a woman or a weapon? My mother, once woman,

now whatever she needs to be: a nuclear family bomb, a forest fire of lost causes,
or perhaps something simpler, like an unkempt garden
my body will return to. My sexuality

is an unmarked grave where someone keeps digging out the headstones, and
I don't know who lays here anymore, in this body,
overgrown with dead things and longing. I guess,
if I'm a hypnotist, that makes me a performer,

And doesn't that serve me right?
I'm a one man production, my life a documentary
of all the ways men can bury themselves, pretend to be other people with a shovel behind
their backs
and still nobody fills the auditorium. I've received praise for being

everything except myself,
as long as there are no monsters at our necks the curtain always lifts

and when I tell my mother, when the musical ends
and I snap my fingers, I worry that she will never wake up from the dream I've created,

that the dead will always remain dead no matter how deeply we love them.
When I wake up from this dream, whose body will I inhabit,

the one writing this poem, or the one underground?
Are these bodies even different?

Symptom

by Yves Olade

after & for Reyna

The remedy for pain is always more pain. There's a logic in that. The way
the radio plays that old song to remind you of autumn. It
takes you back. How much memory makes
everything worse. It comes out of the blue. Everything was red and still on
fire, and what you held came apart in your hands. The rest of the story
catches in your mouth like a hook. It's so soon. You can't open up.
Time has its own axis. Things come around on their own.
Or they don't. *And nothing
lasts forever but the heart,* says the heart. Which is true, for any
given train of thought. The body at the crux of things, holding at the centre.
In spite of this, it was love who died. It was Cain who pulled the trigger. God
marked him up to remind him, and Abel always planned to forget.
And who can blame him? Looking grief in the eye and choosing the other way.
This is how you fold sorrow in on itself.   You let go.
If it comes back to you, it was right all along. Make sure to catch it
close. Like this, there are so many things to do with your hands.
You clap twice and the lights go dark. The radio plays another song. It steals the
silence from your throat. You
don't know what to do with your mouth   when it's empty. But you
have to talk about it now. Teeth snapping shut like a lock. But something leaks out
anyway. Imagine, holding all that blood in your mouth instead of swallowing
it down. Or better yet, spitting it out. If you have something to say,
spit it out. The figure turns left. The road always bends right. And both of us. In the
middle, becoming accidents of ourselves. Here we are:
Driving in circles. Hitting parked cars. Moving in straight
lines and still coming back on ourselves. Getting lost in open fields with
our eyes taped shut. *Where do we go from here?* First, free all the birds from
Eden. You'll find out which way is north. We're turning all the wrong
tricks. So I tell you this one matters. I want to know
if you can say something true and mean it. Try it out: Any

lie is just a story told in the wrong order. Sometimes, we do it on purpose.
We move things around. The lines curve in the dark
like a sphere, so all the sides of history seem infinite.
Really, there's only one. You're a librarian. Putting the words back where they
belong. It's ingenuous. A miracle. You haven't learnt anything at all. You let go
and everything always lands the wrong way up.   You tried so hard
to hold onto the rain. But there are only two sides to touch.
You're always on the wrong one.
Still, I say, *I'm not sorry*. Because I'm not. *Still*, I want to be forgiven. But I don't
want to earn it. Is that what it means to talk about love?
Blood turning lilac when you cut it open?
Look at that heart: Running bright red. Making violence the centre
of things. How it makes such bright mistakes. It doesn't know where
to put them. This too, I think, is a symptom.

Contributors

Manahil Bandukwala is a poet and artist. Her chapbook, "Pipe Rose", came out with *battleaxe press* in 2018. Her work has appeared in the *Puritan, Room Magazine, carte blanche, Coven Editions* and other places. She is currently on the editorial team of *In/Words Magazine* & *Press and Canthius*.

Sherry Bollero is a PhD student and graduate teaching assistant in English at the University of North Dakota where she teaches English composition classes and spends time researching about materialism, adaptation, and Renaissance theater. Recently, she's made the tentative steps toward sharing her creative writing instead of perching on it like a dragon in a cave.

Brittany Coppla graduated from Elon University with a BA in English in May of 2018 and is currently pursuing her MFA in Creative Writing at Sarah Lawrence College. She served as the poetry editor and public relations manager for *Colonnades* during her undergraduate career, and is now working as the online editorial assistant for *Lumina*. Her works have found homes or are forthcoming in *Colonnades, Visions, Asterism, Red Queen,* and more.

Amrita Chakraborty is a Bangladeshi-American writer and student located in New York. Her work has previously been published in *The Rising Phoenix Review, The Olivetree Review* and *Vagabond City*, and is forthcoming in *Winter Tangerine, The Brown Orient,* and *Augur Magazine*. She has also self-published a chapbook entitled "Incarnate". In her free time, Amrita enjoys indie pop music, romantic comedy marathons and stargazing.

Wanda Deglane is a night-blooming desert flower from Arizona. She is the daughter of Peruvian immigrants and attends Arizona State University, pursuing a bachelor's degree in psychology and family & human development. Her poetry has been published by or is forthcoming in *Rust + Moth, Glass: A Journal of Poetry, L'Éphémère Review,* and *Former Cactus*, among other lovely places. Wanda self-published her first poetry book, "Rainlily", in 2018.

Elizabeth Ruth Deyro is a writer, poet, and editor from Laguna, Philippines. She holds a BA in Communication Arts from the University of the Philippines Los Baños. Her artistic work reflects her ever-evolving exploration of identity and interest in themes of religious criticism, psychopathology, philosophy of being, and the woman's body as a political venue. She is the Founding Editor-in-Chief and Creative Director of *The Brown Orient*, and the Prose Editor of *Rag Queen Periodical* and *Red Queen Literary Magazine*. Her work has appeared in or is forthcoming from *Hypertrophic Literary, L'Éphémère Review, Jellyfish Review,* and *Porridge Magazine*, among others.

Logan February is a happy-ish Nigerian owl who likes pizza & typewriters. He is a poet and a book reviewer at *Platypus Press'* Weekend Review. His work has appeared or is forthcoming in *The Adroit Journal*, *wildness*, *Yemassee*, *Raleigh Review*, *Tinderbox Poetry Journal*, and more. He has been nominated for Best of the Net Awards, and his first full length manuscript, "Mannequin in the Nude", was a finalist for the Sillerman First Book Prize for African Poets. He is the author of "How to Cook a Ghost" (*Glass Poetry Press*, 2017), "Painted Blue with Saltwater" (*Indolent Books*, 2018) & "Mannequin in the Nude" (*PANK Books*, 2019).

Sean Glatch is a sophomore studying psychology at the University of Central Florida. He is the author of the chapbook "Late Night Drives" and the literary editor for *Tongue Tied Mag*. Sean's work has been featured in *Rising Phoenix Press*, *Ghost City Review*, *Bombus Press*, and , *L'Éphémère Review*. He has an obsession with the surreal, the uncanny, and the vaguely familiar. You can find more of his work at his blog 7-weeks.tumblr.com.

SK Grout grew up in Auckland, New Zealand and has lived in Frankfurt, Germany and Norwich, England. She splits her time as best she can between London and Auckland. She is the author of the micro chapbook "to be female is to be interrogated" (2018, the poetry annals). Her work also appears in *Landfall*, *Crannóg*, *The Interpreter's House*, *Banshee*, *L'Éphémère Review* and elsewhere. Wanderlust, eco-living, social justice, queer love stories and writing remain priorities of her life. These topics fill most of her twittering at @indeskidge.

Jason Harris is an educator, poet, and visual artist living in Cleveland, Ohio. He is an MFA candidate. His work has appeared or is forthcoming in *Winter Tangerine*, *TRACK//FOUR*, *OCCULUM*, *Riggwelter*, *The Cerurove*, and *Sleeper Service*. He is the Managing Editor of *BARNHOUSE Journal*.

Rachana Hegde is an 18-year-old Indian writer from Hong Kong. Her poetry has appeared in *DIALOGIST*, *Diode Poetry Journal*, and *The Blueshift Journal*. Her work has been recognized by the Scholastic Art and Writing Awards and nominated for Best of the Net. Find her at www.rachanahegde.weebly.com.

Sneha Subramanian Kanta is a GREAT scholarship awardee, and has earned a second postgraduate degree in literature from England. Her chapbook "Home is Hyperbole" won the Boston Uncommon Chapbook Series (*Boston Accent Lit*). She is the founding editor of *Parentheses Journal* and author of "Synecdoche" (*The Poetry Annals*, 2018) and "Prosopopoeia" (*Ghost City Press*, 2018). An old soul, she runs a patisserie.

S.A. Khanum is a writer from the UK.

Amy Kinsman (they/them) is a genderfluid poet and playwright from Manchester, England. As well as being founding editor of *Riggwelter Press* and associate editor of *Three Drops From A Cauldron*, they are also the host of a regular open mic. Their debut pamphlet & was joint-winner of the Indigo Dreams Pamphlet Prize 2017.

Mateo Lara is from Bakersfield, California. He has a chapbook, "X, Marks the Spot" available on Amazon. His poems have been featured in *Orpheus*, *EOAGH*, *Empty Mirror*, and *The New Engagement*. He is an editor for *RabidOak* online literary journal.

Kanika Lawton is a writer, poet, and editor currently living in Toronto, Ontario. She is an MA Candidate at the University of Toronto's Cinema Studies Institute, Editor-in-Chief of *L'Éphémère Review*, and Social Media Manager of *Rambutan Literary*. A two-time Pushcart Prize nominee and 2018 Pink Door Fellow, her work has appeared in *Ricepaper Magazine*, *Vagabond City Literary Journal*, and *Longleaf Review*, among others, and profiled in *The Ellis Review* and *Horn & Ivory Zine*. She is the author of "Wildfire Heart" (*The Poetry Annals*, 2018) and "Loneliness, and Other Ways to Split a Body" (*Ghost City Press*, 2018).

Allegra Lisa left home at sixteen for Interlochen Arts Academy to pursue her passion for writing and to escape familial unrest. She continues to study poetry more closely at Sarah Lawrence. Her script "Unravel" was a quarterfinalist in the *BlueCat Screenplay Competition*, and more of her work can be found in *The Stockholm Review of Literature*, Sarah Lawrence's *The Cliffhanger*, and the 2016 and 2017 issues of *The Interlochen Review*. Allegra is currently putting together a collection of poetry capturing what it feels like for children to grieve when they don't necessarily understand what they are grieving for.

Quinn Lui is a Chinese-Canadian student who wrote this instead of sleeping at what would be considered a reasonable hour. Their work has been published in *L'Éphémère Review*, *Synaesthesia Magazine*, and *Occulum*, among others. You can find them @flowercryptid on Tumblr, Twitter, and Instagram.

Elisávet Makridis is a poet raised in Queens, New York and Greece. Prior to graduating from Sarah Lawrence College, she was the recipient of her alma mater's Andrea Klein Willison Poetry Prize (2015) and Lucy Grealy Prize for Poetry (2016). Her work has been featured in or is forthcoming from *Bellevue Literary Review*, *Tupelo Quarterly* (finalist for the 2018 Poetry Open Prize), *Crab Creek Review, and Frontier Poetry*. She can be found online at elisavetmakridis.com or on Twitter: @elisahvet. Her heart swims somewhere in the Mediterranean.

Yves Olade is a history student who lives in the south of England. He's been featured in *Kingdoms in the Wild*, and published in the *Rising Phoenix Review*, *Bombus Press*, *Glass: A Journal of Poetry*, *Vagabond City Lit* and, *L'Éphémère Review*. Yves also has poetry upcoming in *The Ellis Review*. An avid documentary fan, he loves mobile games, evenings, and lemonade. More of his poetry can be found at yvesolade.tumblr.com or on Twitter @yvesolade.

Rajani Radhakrishnan is from Bangalore, India. Finding time and renewed enthusiasm for poetry after a long career in Financial Applications, she blogs at thotpurge.wordpress.com. Her poems have recently appeared in *The American Poetry Journal*, *The Ekphrastic Review*, *The Calamus Journal* and *The Quiet Letter*.

Kevin A. Risner is writing instructor and ESL Coordinator at the Cleveland Institute of Art. His work can be found in *Rise Up Review*, *Rising Phoenix Review*, *Noble / Gas Qtrly*, *The Wire's Dream*, *Ghost City Review*, and others. He has two short poetry collections published: "My Ear is a Sieve" (*Bottlecap Press*, 2017) and "Lucid" (*The Poetry Annals*, 2018).

Sage is an MFA candidate and COMP fellow at St. Mary's College in California. Their poetry appears/will appear in *FIVE:2:ONE*, *North American Review*, *Penn Review*, *Pittsburgh Poetry Review*, *The Rumpus*, and elsewhere. Find them on Twitter @sagescrittore.

stephanie roberts has work featured and forthcoming in numerous periodicals, and anthologies, including *Verse Daily*, *Arcturus*, *L'Éphémère Review*, *Crannóg Magazine*, *Suitcase of Chrysanthemums*, and *Occulum*. A 2018 Pushcart Prize nominee and recent *Silver Needle Press* Poetry Contest winner, she was born in Central America, grew up in Brooklyn, NY, and now, from a wee French town in Québec, dreams of compassion based society. Her work has been translated into Farsi. Twitter/Instagram @ringtales.

Jen Rouse's poems have appeared in *Poetry*, *The Inflectionist Review*, *Midwestern Gothic*, the *CDC Poetry Project*, *Sinister Wisdom*, *Lavender Review*, *Up the Staircase*, *Parentheses Journal*, *Sliver of Stone*, and elsewhere. She was named a finalist for *the Mississippi Review* 2018 Prize issue and was the winner of the 2017 *Gulf Stream* Summer Contest Issue. Rouse's chapbook, "Acid and Tender", was published in 2016 by *Headmistress Press*.

Saoirse is a junior at Washington College double majoring in English and Sociology with triple minors in creative writing, gender studies and journalism, editing and publishing. She has been writing since she was very young but only started writing in English two years ago. She is always looking for an opportunity to grow as a writer and a reader.

Janelle Salanga is a second-year student at the University of California, Davis, currently studying cognitive science and English. When she's not biking to her favorite coffeeshops, studying, or binge-watching *Brooklyn 99*, she reads poetry for *The Cerurove* and edits the *Kinabukasan Magazine*. Her work has been published or is forthcoming in *The Margins, Occulum, L'Éphémère Review*, and *Tenth Street Miscellany*. She tweets @jvnelly.

Marilyn Schotland is a poet from Philadelphia currently studying for a BA in History of Art at the University of Michigan. She is the recipient of a Hopwood Award. Recent and forthcoming publications can be found in *Cotton Xenomorph, Glass: A Journal of Poetry, Tinderbox Poetry Journal*, and *Five:2:One*.

Mary Sims is an eighteen-year-old poet and writer. She has recently been published *in Kingdoms of the Wild, Moonchild Magazine, Mooky Chick, Anti-Heroin Chic, Rising Phoenix Press*, and *Anatolios Magazine*. She is currently working towards earning her BA in English, and spends her days dreaming of writing beloved poetry while living in the mountains with her friends and family close by.

Kwan-Ann Tan is a nineteen-year-old writer from Malaysia who is currently studying at Oxford University. When she isn't waxing about Woolf & waning on Joyce, she can be found on Twitter at @KwanAnnTan.

Chandler Veilleux, formerly known as Chelsie, is a transgender poet and an MFA candidate at New England College. Previous publications can be found in *Vagabond City Lit, sidereal*, and *Impossible Archetype*.

Aaron White holds an MA in Literary Studies from Eastern Illinois University and contributes to *Bluestem Magazine* as an assistant nonfiction editor. His work has appeared in *Mothers Always Write, Parent Co, 13th Dimension, Prong & Posy, The Pedestal Magazine*, and other publications. He spends his days raising a toddler, navigating academia, trying to sell a novel, and wallowing in obscurity. Connect with him on Twitter @amwhite90 and Tumblr at amwhite90.tumblr.com.

Nicole Yurcaba, a Ukrainian-American writer, teaches in Bridgewater College's English department, where she also serves as the Assistant Director for the Bridgewater International Poetry Festival. Her poems and essays appear journals such as *The Atlanta Review, The Lindenwood Review, Chariton Review, Still: The Journal, OTHER., Junto Magazine*, and many others. When she is not teaching, writing, or traveling, or dancing to Depeche Mode and Wolfsheim in goth clubs, Yurcaba lives, gardens, and fishes in West Virginia with her fiancé on their mountain homestead.

What is love? What is desire? How do they look and why do we feel them? *The Anatomy of Desire* brings together poets whose unflinching honesty seeks to answer these questions and does so in a rich variety of style and tone. Moving from love to loss, romance to family, this anthology unwraps love in all its forms, and forces us to question our instincts and emotions as we identify our own pasts and presents through its poetry. The poems in *The Anatomy of Desire* share more than just their passionate theme; a sense of urgency, desperation, pervades the collection as poets attempt to articulate the impossible feeling of desire. The desperate struggle is ultimately a successful one, resulting in a diverse anthology which deconstructs tropes of love and reconstructs it on poets' own terms, resulting in poetry which beautifully says the unsayable.

— **Martha O'Brien,** poet at the University of Cardiff.

It takes a startling amount of bravery to let yourself bleed poetry onto the page in the way that the poets in *The Anatomy of Desire* have done. You feel their bitterness, pain, and longing vividly, despite the shortness of many of the works. Although the subjects of each poem are incredibly different, the thread that ties them together is raw emotion, and it's necessary to pause whilst reading the anthology to fully absorb what can be difficult to read in some cases; often because we understand exactly what the poems mean, because we have lived them too. Crossing boundaries of gender, sexuality, and nationality, the anthology reminds us of what it is to be human in a myriad of different ways. A truly beautiful piece of literature.

— **Simone Fraser,** poet at the University of Oxford.

The poems in this anthology offer a poignant and incisive look at the human condition. The multifaceted nature of the curated works have the gift of breaking and also possess the power of healing. The anthology is a mix of intercontinental voices drawn from the primary need for telling a story and leading the reader into their minds and bodies.

It is amazing how contemporary poets are modifying the meaning of poetry and it is gratifying when agreeing that the ones in this book have outdone themselves.

—**Michael Akuchie**, Contributing Editor at Barren Magazine.

The Anatomy of Desire is an anthology of myriad voices. It is the juxtaposition of several perspectives, styles, and thoughts. From an erasure poem created out of a poem by Rilke, to descriptions of daily experiences, and complexities of identity, this anthology has it all. There is a tenderness that accompanies these poems, offering an engaging company to the reader.

The stylistic nuances of these poems are compelling. Each poet shines with their intriguing narrative—and this is an anthology recommended for all readers of literature.

Intricate and rich, these offerings demand to be reread and sung—in the unique voices of diverse realities they offer. The multiplicities in the narratives and voices are what makes the experience of reading each poem fascinating. Readers may expect to be left with a sense of bewilderment and intrigue after having read the anthology. *The Anatomy of Desire* is proof of what a small press may offer with its authenticity and diverse integration of voices.

The anthology is emblematic of a song that demands to be sung, of narratives that find their utterance, all with fine poets sending out their narratives into the world. The poems in this anthology are urgent, and each offers a world of their own. A must read.

— **Harshal Desai**. Founding Editor, *Parentheses Journal.*

The poems in *The Anatomy of Desire* will force you to take a breath between each piece as if it were you, the reader, at the bottom of a pool or in a passionate kiss alongside the speakers. The poets in this anthology will take you through computer code and city skylines and leave you wanting. These poems go beyond the physicality of desire and delve into the deeply emotional, yearning sentiments behind it. On one page, you'll be awash in the imagery and tactility of a scene, then on the next, you'll be entrenched in an intangible emotion. *The Anatomy of Desire* takes you from the open sky to a fire deep within the earth, yet basks in a grounded, painful reality. It takes you through time and space, through seasons, from childhood to adulthood, and into history and the future. These poems are without question some of the best I've read in some time and become all the more powerful put together here. This anthology balances trauma and pain with love, lust, and longing to craft a collection that will stay with you long after you've read its final page.

— **Juliette Sebock**, author of "Mistakes Were Made" (2017) and Founding Editor of *Nightingale & Sparrow.*

Desire can be a fast-burning flame. In these poems, it is so much more: a wrestling match with grief, a lifelong bond with family, a fear, a humiliation, a question, a reverence, a revolution. The poets in this collection have taken private and sacred memories and turned them in their strong hands in the daylight for us. Sudden madness can threaten: "why can i not haunt you like this," Amrita Chakraborty asks in "roanoke," "why can i not will these fingers into talons"? Or a struggle for survival can be sustained in a different way, like an endangered butterfly's "mouth part filling heart with nectar, / where she is not supposed to exist," stephanie roberts says in "My Timeline is Glad." These poems are curated together in such a way that they seem to reflect each other at the sides and blend in at the edges. You want them in you.

-- **Tucker Lieberman**, author of "Painting Dragons" (2018).

"Intricate and rich, these offerings demand to be reread and sung—in the unique voices of diverse realities they offer."

— Harshal Desai, Founding Editor of the *Parentheses Journal*.

"a sense of urgency [and] desperation, pervades the collection."

— Martha O'Brien, poet at the University of Cardiff.

"Desire can be a fast-burning flame. In these poems, it is so much more: a wrestling match with grief, a lifelong bond with family, a fear, a humiliation, a question, a reverence, a revolution."

— Tucker Lieberman, author of "Painting Dragons" (2018).

"a poignant and incisive look at the human condition."

— Michael Akuchie, Contributing Editor at *Barren Magazine*.

"It takes a startling amount of bravery to let yourself bleed poetry onto the page in the way that [these] poets have done."

— Simone Fraser, poet at the University of Oxford.

"This anthology balances trauma and pain with love, lust, and longing to craft a collection that will stay with you long after you've read its final page."

— Juliette Sebock, author of "Mistakes Were Made" (2017) and Founding Editor of *Nightingale & Sparrow*.

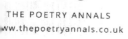

THE POETRY ANNALS
www.thepoetryannals.co.uk

CPSIA information can be obtained
at www.ICGtesting.com
Printed in the USA
FSHW022017290119
55356FS

9 780244 695644